IMAGES
of England

CHALFONT ST PETER
AND GERRARDS CROSS

IMAGES
of England

CHALFONT ST PETER
AND GERRARDS CROSS

Colin J. Seabright

TEMPUS

A more standard composite card, with five views of Chalfont St Peter in a decorative surround, this was posted in 1907.

Frontispiece: An early multi-view postcard offering exceptional value for money! Eleven real photographic miniatures of Gerrards Cross for the price of one postcard in 1905.

First published 2002
Copyright © Colin J. Seabright, 2002

Tempus Publishing Limited
The Mill, Brimscombe Port,
Stroud, Gloucestershire, GL5 2QG

ISBN 0 7524 2493 7

Typesetting and origination by
Tempus Publishing Limited
Printed in Great Britain by
Midway Colour Print, Wiltshire

Contents

Live in the Country!

—— WHY NOT CHOOSE ——

BEAUTIFUL, BRACING, BEECHY BUCKS?

GERRARD'S CROSS
AS A RESIDENTIAL DISTRICT.

View of Common, showing Pond.

A DELIGHTFUL RURAL CENTRE. ✛ ✛ ✛ ✛
✛ ✛ ✛ RICH IN NATURAL CHARMS ✛ ✛ ✛
✛ ✛ ✛ ✛ ✛ ☞ HISTORICAL ASSOCIATIONS

This is the front page of an Estate Agent's brochure extolling the virtues of Gerrards Cross as a place to live, in about 1910.

Introduction

This little volume illustrates the twentieth century development of two adjacent, but very different villages in the county of Buckinghamshire; Chalfont St Peter with a thousand years of recorded history including reference in the Domesday Book to Horn Hill, Chalfont Common and Austenwood in addition to Chalfont St Peter itself, and Gerrards Cross, only created 150 years ago. Despite their differences, their recent histories are closely linked as, until the middle of the nineteenth century, Chalfont St Peter included most of the area we now know as Gerrards Cross village. Gerrards Cross parish was then created out of five neighbouring parishes, Chalfont St Peter, Fulmer, Iver, Langley Marish and Upton, whose boundaries met on Gerrards Cross Common, or as it was originally known, Chalfont Heath.

Stone Age flints have been found near the Misbourne and a pre-historic Plateau Camp or hill fort covering twenty-two acres, the largest in the county, is situated in Bulstrode Park. A collection of Roman coins was dug up near Gold Hill, but there is no evidence of any permanent early settlements in the district.

In the middle ages, Chalfont St Peter was more closely associated with its neighbour on the other side, Chalfont St Giles, and the two were lumped together simply as Celfunde, and first noted separately in the Domesday Book, when the Manor of Chalfont belonged to Bishop Odo. It later passed to Missenden Abbey, and after the reformation was sold to the Bulstrodes whose family name is said to originate from an incident soon after the Norman conquest, when, mounted on bulls, they and their supporters, including the Hampdens, prevented the King's men from seizing their estate.

In 1229 King Henry III granted Chalfont St Peter a weekly market on Wednesdays and an annual fair on the eve and festival of Saints Peter and Paul. The market faded away, but the 1867 directory recorded an annual fair for pedlary and toys on the 4th and 5th of September.

The infamous Judge Jeffreys, the barbaric 'hanging Judge', features in the history of both places. In 1675 he purchased the vast Bulstrode Estate, beside the Oxford Road, and in the following year an army of builders erected a mansion there, using the materials from an older house on the site. Ten years later, Bulstrode was badly damaged by fire and he moved to The Grange at Chalfont St Peter while it was being rebuilt, and during his stay there set up his court in a room at the nearby Greyhound Inn. Jeffreys already knew the area well from visits to his cousin, Sir John Turner, a previous owner of The Grange. Bulstrode was later owned by Hans Bentinck who had the formal gardens laid out, also straightened the Windsor Road where it crossed his land between The Packhorse and the turning to Hedgerly. Under the ownership of his successors, the Dukes of Portland, Bulstrode became one of England's greatest houses, with an extensive menagerie in the beautiful grounds. At the beginning of the nineteenth century they employed Humphrey Repton to reshape the gardens and park and James Wyatt to build a new house. Only part of the South Front had been rebuilt when a change in the family fortune caused work to slow, then stop altogether for fifty years, and what remains of this house now belongs to the World Ecumenical Crusade.

At the other end of the district, the Manor of Brudenells, with the estate and mansion then known as Old Place, later as Chalfont House or Park, passed through various families to the Hibberts at the beginning of the nineteenth century, when Chalfont Park was described as a fine and extensive demesne, undulating and beautifully timbered, including the oldest and largest ash-tree in England. The Hibbert family were great benefactors to the village throughout the nineteenth and early twentieth centuries, their gifts including land for allotments and the cottage hospital.

Until 1859, Gerrards Cross existed only as a cross-roads in the middle of a common, not then on the original spot since both roads had been slightly diverted early in that century, but after the construction of St James Church, built to serve the residents of the outlying parts of five parishes the new parish of Gerrards Cross was created out of these parishes, but mostly from Chalfont St Peter.

Chalfont St Peter was a well-established village by that date with an ancient church, rebuilt 150 years earlier, and was a flourishing rural community with a good selection of shops and other tradesmen. For the whole of Victoria's reign, Chalfont St Peter was the dominant partner, with a population in 1891 totalling 1,500 compared with only 600 in Gerrards Cross. From its opening in 1894, the Chalfont Colony for Epileptics at Chalfont Common was an important feature of Chalfont St Peter as, for many years, the staff and patients made up around 10 per cent of the village's total population.

After the opening of the railway in 1906, development followed rapidly, mainly at Gerrards Cross, but also, to a lesser extent and rather later, at Chalfont St Peter. A 1910 guide to *Where to Live around London* notes that;

'Gerrards Cross is a new residential district opened up since the advent of the Great Western and Great Central joint railway. The situation is delightful and very healthy and residences - all of a good class – are rapidly being built, and are in great demand. To meet the requirements of the new and increasing population, there are already, near the station, a telegraph office, hotel, 3 banks and excellent shops of various kinds. A little to the west of the station is the large breezy common across which is seen the parish church. The surrounding district is full of unspoiled natural beauty and is particularly rich in those beech trees for which the county is famous. Chalfont St Peter, a mile from Gerrards Cross, is a quaint old–fashioned place.'

Gerrards Cross grew because it combined the amenities of country life with the provision of town shopping facilities. The railway encouraged travel with the very reasonable fares to London of four shillings (twenty pence) return first class, or two shillings third class. With an annual season ticket then costing only £20 first class, Gerrards Cross rapidly grew into a commuter village, or small town, and soon overtook its neighbour in size and, although residents of Chalfont St Peter would probably disagree, in importance.

Despite its rural situation and olde–worlde atmosphere, Chalfont St Peter was well ahead of all the surrounding towns in one respect with a cinema, The Palace, remotely situated in Grove Lane, at the top of Gold Hill, as early as 1914.

The heart of Chalfont St Peter remained unchanged until the twenties, when the new shopping area of Market Place was created in Gold Hill Lane. Another period of development in the late twenties and thirties in both villages resulted in some erosion of the open space between them. Also in the thirties the first wave of demolition hit Chalfont St Peter with a clearance order on the historic cottages of Barrack Yard between the High Street and the river, which were so named since Judge Jefferys troop of bodyguards was stationed there while he lived at The Grange.

Much more destruction was to come thirty years later, when road works to ease the traffic flow on the Amersham to Uxbridge main road brought wholesale demolition of the outer part of Chalfont St Peter towards Gravel Hill. Also in the sixties, more of the High Street was replaced by a concrete shopping precinct, finally destroying the historic rural atmosphere in what a local author recently described as 'A Lost Village', while further residential development has created one large conurbation from the two separate villages.

Accurate dating of the pictures on postcards is extremely difficult even when they bear a postmark, therefore the dates given for the majority of the illustrations must be taken as informed estimates, mostly accurate to within five years.

One
River Misbourne

The Mill Pond and Splash, Chalfont St. Peter.

After meandering through the fields of Chalfont St Giles, the Misbourne, a typically intermittent chalk stream, was dammed at its approach to Chalfont St Peter to form a mill-pond. The mill, originally built to grind corn, powered a blanket factory in the nineteenth century, but had completely disappeared by the twentieth, leaving only the old mill-pond, sheltered by the distant trees, and the overflow waterfall. Pictured here in about 1908, the mill's tail-stream naturally proved an irresistible attraction for the children of the village.

The Misbourne River, Chalfont St. Peter.   2445

Slightly further downstream, the river is pictured in about 1960, when demolition had started for the widening of the Amersham Road. Children were still able to enjoy the pleasures of a rural stream before it was edged with modern buildings, including the 1962 Community Centre on the former Mill Meadow.

The Misbourne then divided, flowing partly behind and partly underneath the Greyhound Inn, re-forming as it entered the open space in front of the church. Pictured here at the turn of the century, the stream was then crossed by a foot-bridge outside the pub, which was reflected in the still, shallow water.

Seen from the Vicarage gateway beside the end of the foot-bridge at about the same date, the stream flowed across the wide street to another footbridge on the far side, before passing between the old buildings there.

A few years later and a horse-drawn trap is just entering the ford, then the only way for vehicles to cross the Misbourne. When the first cars started using the road, many became waterlogged, and the village butcher, next door to the George Inn, kept a strong rope at the ready to help pull them out.

THE VILLAGE, CHALFONT ST. PETER.

In about 1910 a road bridge was provided over the stream, which still formed a pond across the other half of the square, seen here in about 1920 with a pair of horses cooling off in the water.

The Village, Chalfont St. Peter.   SPAULL & Co., GERRARDS CROSS.

A 1920 view across the rather depleted Misbourne to the George with its rustic seats outside, this also includes the railings of the churchyard. Seven years later, the river was buried in a culvert beneath the tarmac of the widened street.

From the centre of the village the Misbourne passed behind the cottages of Barrack Yard and into open country where it divided again, around Willows Island, still within view of the church. This postcard was published in about 1905.

Just beyond the island, the re-united stream was bridged by this wooden structure carrying a foot-path which ran from the High Street to Hogtrough Wood and Chalfont Lodge. All this stretch of the river is now buried beneath the Chalfont St Peter bypass.

The Misbourne next enters Chalfont Park where it passes behind the house. Here it is again dammed to form a decorative lake, pictured in about 1905, with neat lawns reaching from the house to the water's edge, where there was also a small boat-house.

A small wooded island divides the half-mile long lake in half. This 1925 photograph is of the lower section, with the island at the right edge of the view and the dam out of sight to the left.

A popular subject with photographers, this 1925 postcard shows the waterfall where the surplus water flows over the dam at the bottom end of Chalfont Park's artificial lake.

A second, shallower branch of the river bypassed the lake and fed watercress beds between the house and the village. Before re-joining the main stream, it was crossed by a footpath through a rather muddy ford, pictured here in about 1910.

15

As the river leaves Chalfont Park it is crossed by a solid plank bridge carrying the footpath linking Lower Road with Chalfont Lodge and Mopes Farm, near the edge of the parish and West Hyde, over the county border into Hertfordshire.

From Chalfont Park, the Misbourne veers across to the Hertfordshire side of the wide valley where it passes under the railway viaduct on its way to join the larger River Colne at Denham, eventually to flow into the Thames.

Two

The Oxford Road

This chapter looks at the section of the main London to Oxford Road within the parish of Gerrards Cross, illustrating some of the places of interest along this historic highway in sequence from East to West. Mayne Reid, the eccentric author of boys' adventure stories, returned from fighting in Mexico and built The Rancho, a Mexican-style house on a wooded site on the south side of the Oxford Road near Tatling End. Although construction was never completed, he lived there from 1860-1866, when financial difficulties, due to his extravagant life-style, forced him to return to the United States. The half-finished house fell derelict and was later demolished. This drawing of the house and lodges was published in about 1895, when one of the lodges was all that remained.

Slightly nearer the Common on the other side of the Oxford Road, and by the nineteenth milestone from London, Woodside, a seventeenth century house largely rebuilt in the eighteenth, is thought to have been originally a coaching inn. This photograph of the house, with the main road just out of sight to the left, was sent by the owners as a Christmas card in 1907.

This 1900 view is along the muddy Oxford Road from just after Woodhill, looking past the block of three houses near the corner of Fulmer Road towards The French Horn.

Taken by a visitor on a Sunday in 1912, before Sunday motoring had become the national pastime, this view from the forecourt of The French Horn shows the featureless expanse of Common beside the Oxford Road toward the cross-roads.

THE FRENCH HORN, GERRARDS CROSS.

Twenty years later, the well-surfaced and curbed Oxford Road, by then recognized by the Ministry of Transport as a trunk road and known as the A40, still carried surprisingly little traffic apart from the three visitors to The French Horn.

This 1920 aerial view was photographed from above the Oxford Road looking west past the French Horn towards Gerrards Cross church. To the left of the pub its extensive stable yard reached the edge of the view. Immediately beyond the pub forecourt, the small group of roadside buildings included a shop, a tea-room, and the police station. The patch of dense woodland between there and the church was cleared a few years later to make way for a line of houses facing the scrubby edge of the Common.

Opposite: In this late twenties photograph the Automobile Association patrol–man is making use of the telephone facilities in the AA box at the cross-roads of the Windsor and Oxford Roads.

Looking back from opposite the Bull Hotel in about 1900 the common is seen to be open, flat and treeless, covered only with gorse and heather which had developed after grazing ceased. Ten years later, fires destroyed all the gorse, and wind-borne silver-birch seeds changed the aspect to one of light woodland.

Post Office and West End, Gerrards Cross.

This 1900 view from an upstairs window of The Bull, looking over its lodge and across the Oxford Road, shows the nucleus of the original Gerrards Cross including its Post Office.

Another 1920 aerial photograph, this shows the Bull Hotel with its maze of outbuildings on one side of the Oxford Road, and the other old buildings of Gerrards Cross on the other. Curving away from the Bull's forecourt, the drive leads through the trees of Bulstrode Park to the mansion, well over half a mile away. Shortly after this photograph was taken, parts of the park behind the Bull were given over to the development of large houses.

Pictured in 1907, Gerrards Cross Post Office was housed in the annexe to this cottage beside the Oxford Road until it moved to a new building in Packhorse Road in 1912. Although only a sub-office it handled mail from the surrounding villages as well as the three letter-boxes in Gerrards Cross, at the station, the cross-roads, and down the Windsor Road by the Hedgerley turning, all cleared three times a day.

After its long straight run across Gerrards Cross Common, the Oxford Road dips between trees to start its twisting way to Beaconsfield. It was pictured in 1900 beside the gates of Wood Bank, the home of Sam Fay, the General Manager of the Great Central Railway, who, following his own advertising, had moved into the area.

Three
Refreshment

THE "DUMB BELL",
HORN HILL,
CHALFONT ST PETER.
"*FULLY LICENCED*"

Chalfont St Peter and Gerrards Cross have always had several establishments offering food, drink, and accommodation to visitors. This chapter illustrates a selection of the many public houses, hotels, and restaurants, taken in geographical sequence, starting with the extreme edge of Chalfont St Peter and ending with the coaching inns along the Oxford Road in Gerrards Cross. Horn Hill is the north-eastern part of Chalfont St Peter, and the Dumb Bell is actually on the parish and county boundary, overlooking the Colne Valley. Published in about 1930, this card shows various scenes in the pub's garden, then partly laid out as a model village.

Coming down off the hills and on to the main Amersham Road, 'The Wheatleys', originally a farm, opened in 1905 as a 'cyclists' rest, with a lunch and tea pavilion in a hundred acres of beech wood, only twenty-one miles from Marble Arch'. In 1930, after selling off some of the land, it advertised as 'a comfortable home with every modern convenience in a 200 year old oak timbered house, standing in own grounds of two acres', offering choice bedrooms at three guineas a week. This photograph is of the road frontage when still a farm.

The second view of 'The Wheatleys' is one from a set of six postcards published in about 1907, shortly after it opened as a guest house. Its grounds included a tennis court, lawns with deck chairs, and woodland, where rope swings hung from the convenient branches.

Entering the village from the Amersham Road and Gravel Hill, the first public house was the Rose and Crown, which had a yard and outbuildings backing on to the Misbourne. This advertising card was published shortly after the pub was rebuilt on this site in 1903. It was demolished in the sixties for road realignment.

This 1907 photograph shows the next pub, The Kings Arms, on the corner of Joiners Lane, facing the yard of The Greyhound. This was another of the village's many attractive and historic buildings sacrificed in the sixties in the interest of traffic.

Within the image, handwritten caption:

REYHOUND INN, CHALFONT-ST-PETER, BUCKS., AD:1062
MOUS COACHING HOUSE. WITH JUDGE JEFFREY'S COURT ROOM
ILT EARLY 17TH CENTURY; GEORGE THE THIRD'S BED; AND
TURIES OLD TIMBER   A.A., RAC.

We come next to the most well-known building in Chalfont St Peter, The Greyhound Inn. This 1930 postcard of the pub's yard also includes a potted history of the Inn, though not entirely accurate. The Greyhound, a typical English coaching inn, was built in 1577, and the infamous Judge Jeffreys, while living locally, held his court in one of its upstairs rooms a century later. Until the twenties a line of stables and outhouses separated the yard from the adjacent road, and coaches came and went via the central arch, emerging in the High Street beside the stream in front of the church. The Inn's attractive position, partly over the Misbourne, has recently been its downfall, when severe flooding in late 2000 put it out of action for the whole of 2001.

This card of the interior of The Greyhound, published for the proprietors in the late forties, shows the ancient brick fireplace and low-beamed ceiling of the pub's cosy lounge.

The Greyhound Inn, Chalfont St. Peter.

CSP.I

The yard is pictured again in the late fifties, when the archway had been filled in for use as a dining room, and the creeper had completely taken over the streamside wing. A yellow and black stage coach had been parked in the yard for nearly twenty years to remind visitors of the Inn's coaching past.

Next door to the church and behind The Greyhound was the early Victorian vicarage, on a site occupied since the thirteenth century when its fish-pond was created by damming a small branch of the Misbourne. From 1911 the incumbent lived elsewhere in the village, and The Old Vicarage was opened as a guest house until the sixties. This view over the pond was sent by a guest in 1916.

On the other side of the wide High Street, The George, another coaching inn, faces the church across the Misbourne. Pictured in 1930, after the road bridge had removed the necessity to ford the stream, the seventeenth century George still retained its coach arch, offering 'Good Stabling' in the rear yard.

Further along the High Street, this short length included three pubs when pictured in 1905. On the left, The Carpenters Arms was one of a line of fifteenth and sixteenth century cottages, all later demolished and replaced in 1966 by a concrete shopping precinct. Beyond these, on the bend and facing The White Hart, another cottage beer-house, The Bakers Arms, was rebuilt and enlarged in the thirties.

The front of The White Hart is pictured here in about 1970. This small village hostelry, which opened before 1750 and is said to be haunted, has changed little in appearance in the last century.

Chalfont Park Hotel, Gerrards Cross.

High Street leads into Lower Road and to Chalfont Park. After centuries of private ownership, the Estate opened as a hotel in 1922. Pictured a year or two later, it offered 'Fine Lounge, Reception, Billiard and Dining Rooms and a Ballroom', and advertised as 'A Capital Rendezvous for a Weekend Motoring Run', twenty miles from London.

The Hotel made a feature of its 300 acre grounds, which included both hard and grass tennis courts, and a golf course, 'where mid-week golfers will find an excellent course combined with picturesque and quiet surroundings'. Another feature of the grounds was this Italian Garden, laid out by Lutyens and Jekyll in 1912, photographed in the twenties.

Among the out-buildings, the castellated stable block had been converted into the hotel's garage, pictured in the mid–twenties when it provided all requirements for guests' vehicles. During the Second World War, the hotel became a convalescent home for wounded servicemen, and in 1944 the complete estate was bought by the British Aluminium Company for use as a research centre, and laboratory blocks were built in place of the kitchen garden and out-buildings.

Returning to the centre of Chalfont St Peter, the historic Grange, in the angle between the High Street and Gold Hill became a hotel for a short while in the mid–twenties. This 1927 view down the slope of Gold Hill Common includes the main entrance to The Grange Hotel and its garage, at the right edge of the picture.

At the top of Gold Hill Common, the Victorian 'Jolly Farmer' dispensed refreshment for nearly a century until demolished in 1965 and replaced by a larger modern building alongside. When pictured, in 1920, the publican's family also ran the stores and tearooms next door, at the end of a short parade of shops.

Previously the home of Major-General Prior, a breeder of King Charles Spaniels, the late Victorian Ethorpe House then became a long term residential hotel with a public 'Tea-Room' in its extensive grounds. By 1924, with much of its land sold for building, it became the Ethorpe Hotel, pictured here in 1930.

Pictured again in 1950, The Ethorpe Hotel had changed very little over the years, and is still flourishing today, though now with car parking in place of some of the flower-beds.

Almost opposite the Ethorpe on a wedge-shaped site at the corner of Oak End Way and South Park, The Park Creamery opened in about 1910, selling 'Pure Rich Milk delivered twice daily from our own herd of Jersey and Kerry Cows at Chalfont Park.'

In addition to selling milk and dairy products, the Park Creamery served 'teas and light refreshments in a picturesque reproduction of an Old English Thatched House'. While the outside may have been old-world thatched, this card shows that the interior was stylishly modern.

Behind the serving counter and butter display in the previous view was the butter-making area with its power-driven churns. These pictures are from a set of postcards published by a Southall photographer in around 1920.

The final card goes right back to the source, with a view of some of the dairy's cattle in their field at the Denham end of Chalfont Park. The creamery was demolished and replaced by an estate agency in the fifties, but the farm remains, now crossed by the M25.

At the other end of Gerrards Cross shopping centre is the Inn after which the main street is named. The original Packhorse Inn, together with an adjacent forge, was built in 1708, and until the Great War each publican doubled as blacksmith. The present building is a modern replacement, pictured here in the early fifties.

Beside the Oxford Road at the eastern end of the common, The Apple Tree has had a long history as a place of refreshment. Originally The Fox and Hounds, after a period as a private house it became The Apple Tree Corner Tea Rooms from about 1930. The interior of The Apple Tree Restaurant is pictured here in the late forties, long before it became part of the Beefeater chain.

THE FRENCH HORN, GERRARDS CROSS, BUCKS.
THE WELL KNOWN NIGHT HOUSE BETWEEN OXFORD & LONDON.

The old French Horn on the Oxford Road is pictured here in 1906, displaying posters and timetables for the new railway service which was soon to finish off most of the remaining horse traffic. Until well after The Great War, this 'well-known night house' kept exceptional hours with a special licence to cater for the needs of the carters of market garden produce on their way to Covent Garden Market at dead of night.

Another picture of The French Horn from the early years of the twentieth century, but with a rather different class of horse transport on the forecourt - the local scrap merchant. The Inn was replaced by a much larger building after the Second World War.

At the other end of the common, the imposing frontage of The Bull Hotel faces the common across a very muddy Oxford Road in this 1900 view. Highwaymen were a well-known danger on the wild stretch of the Oxford Road between Uxbridge and Beaconsfield, and tradition holds that some of the worst offenders were actually based here, a tradition maintained by naming a bar after the infamous Jack Shrimpton.

The Bull was built in 1688, incorporating old timbers from the original Bulstrode mansion nearby. It was first known as The Oxford Arms, but the sign showing that city's heraldic device, a standing bull, led to the inn's at first unofficial, revised name. It was photographed here in about 1912, with both horse-drawn and motorised transport outside.

In about 1915, the section to the left of the original three-storey block looks rather neglected, but guests at that time commented on the high standard of the rooms and beautiful gardens.

Bull Hotel, Gerrards Cross.

After the Great War, the Bull closed as a hotel while it housed tenants of the neighbouring Bulstrode Estate. Pictured in the thirties, the re-opened Bull, with extensions at both ends providing more bedrooms, a ballroom and a 'West End' restaurant, boasted one of the longest frontages among English Inns.

Four
Religion

This chapter illustrates a few of the churches and chapels in Chalfont St Peter and Gerrards Cross, lack of space preventing inclusion of more than a selection of the most historic or interesting buildings. By far the oldest foundation in the area is the Parish Church which gave Chalfont St Peter the second part of its name a thousand years ago. The original flint and chalk-stone building was almost totally destroyed in 1708 when the tower, already suffering from neglect, collapsed through the roof of the nave during a severe storm. The 1714 replacement, 'a very ugly brick-built church', was then remodelled and enlarged in 1852. The church is seen through its 1800 iron railings on this 1905 postcard.

Now a closer look at the church which was described in a guide of 1860 as 'an admirable adaptation of a hideous red brick church of the last century'. This thirties photograph of the tower end shows clearly the brickwork with its corner stones, reported to have come from the ruins of Roman Verulamium at St Albans.

The interior of the church with its hanging oil lamps is pictured here in 1905. Many of the ancient brasses from the old church, the oldest dating from 1388, were re-mounted in the new building.

In 1866 a chapel-of-ease to the main Chalfont St Peter Parish church was built at Horn Hill on the high ground north of the village. Almost on the county boundary, it was built to seat about sixty worshippers who had previously had a long hilly walk to the centre of the village and back. It is pictured in about 1950.

The Baptist chapel was built in 1870 on the highest corner of Gold Hill Common, on the site of an Independent Meeting-House opened in 1792. The chapel, pictured in 1910, was described in a County Guide of 1898 as 'an ugly chapel suggestive of an inartistic dolls-house'.

This view of the back of Gerrards Cross Parish church was published in about 1900. Twentieth century opinion of this Victorian novelty in ecclesiastical architecture has not been very flattering, varying from 'strangely foreign in a lovely English setting', to 'of eccentric design, to looking like the pumping-station of a waterworks'.

This view of the front of Gerrards Cross church was photographed from the path across the Common in about 1930. The church had been built in 1859 in memory of Major-General Alexander Reid by his spinster sisters. They employed architect William Tite, who spent six months in Italy gaining inspiration. It is said that one of the sisters insisted on a dome and the other on a tower, so the church was built with both, and its silhouette was often described as reminiscent of an old steam-engine.

Construction of St Joseph's church in Austen Wood Lane was started in 1913 by a group of Carmelites who had extended their teaching area into south Buckinghamshire five years earlier. The incomplete building opened for services in 1914 and was used in its unfinished state, pictured in the thirties, until completion and extension in 1962/3.

The Lady Altar and Memorial Chapel, St. Joseph's, Gerrards Cross

The interior of the incomplete St Joseph's church is pictured here in the twenties. In his architectural guide to Buckinghamshire, Nikolaus Pevsner described St Josephs as 'A barn of a brick church in simplified Gothic Style'.

Built in 1922 next to the Post Office in Station Parade, Gerrards Cross, and pictured a few years later, the Congregational church is one of the few local churches not to have been the subject of adverse criticism.

Pictured in about 1950, Swarthmore, still a fairly new house, then belonged to the Swarthmore Housing Society. With later extensions to the building it is still a residential home, and also the Sunday meeting place.

Five
Education

The first proper schools in the district were the Church of England schools at Chalfont St Peter and Gerrards Cross, established in the seventeenth and nineteenth centuries respectively. Following the opening of the railway through the district, several private schools catered for the greatly increased population from about 1910, with several more newly opened or transferred from London in the thirties. This chapter illustrates the buildings of several of these schools in the approximate order of opening in the area. The very first was Chalfont St Peter Church School, initially housed in Church House, on the corner of the churchyard. In 1846 a purpose-built school opened in Lambscroft Lane, which was then re-named School Lane. Around the start of the twentieth century, firstly the girls and later the boys transferred to the buildings they still occupy in Church Lane. This photograph from around 1910 shows a group of the girls in the 'new' building.

Pictured in 1900, Gerrards Cross Church School was next on the scene, built in 1861, soon after the church. Initially with just one classroom for about forty pupils, it more than doubled after the 1870 Education Act, and, extended several times to meet the growing demand, the School remained in use for over a century.

Seen again in 1908 with a group of pupils on the edge of the Common, the Victorian building was demolished after the school's move to new premises in Moreland Drive, and was replaced by Colston Court, a block of apartments named after the school's popular headmaster from 1879 - 1920.

Opposite: One of the first private schools catering for the increasing post-railway population of Gerrards Cross, Cranley Court advertised in a Great Central Railway guide of 1910.

Cranley Court

North Park, GERRARD'S CROSS.

First-class ————
Boarding and
Day School
————For GIRLS

For Prospectus apply Principal.

The School founded on Modern Principles of Educational Science is especially arranged to combine the most Modern Educational Requirements with the comfort and refinements of home life. ⚜ Large and Fully Qualified Staff.

This card, posted by one of the girls in 1911, shows some of the Cranley Court pupils at drill in front of the school's main building. The school continued until the thirties, after which the North Park building reverted to residential use, later becoming the first Chiltern Cheshire Home.

Another card with a 1911 postmark, this shows the first premises of Gayhurst School, a large house with classroom annexe, in Milton Avenue.

GAYHURST SCHOOL GERRARD'S CROSS

Head Master: C. C. S. GIBBS, M.C., M.A.

NEW SCHOOL BUILDINGS — VIEW FROM BULL LANE.

A Corner of Playing Fields.

The Swimming Bath.

The Switchback Railway.

The Workshop.

GAYHURST SCHOOL prepares boys between the ages of 6 and 14 for the Public Schools. The School Bus meets boys who come by train at the Station and also collects them from other districts.

In the mid-twenties Gayhurst School moved to larger premises in Bull Lane, as shown in this advertisement from the 1930 Homeland Guide to the 'Chalfont Country'. The school has remained there to this day.

Maltmans Green, originally a modest farmhouse, but greatly extended for the wealthy Drummond family of bankers in 1883, was bought in 1911 by another private school catering for the new residents of Gerrards Cross, and still provides this service. This card was posted by a pupil in 1944.

Chalfont Lodge was situated in extensive grounds on the hillside above Chalfont Park, to which estate it originally belonged. In about 1930 it became a girls' school with a wide range of outdoor activities, including an open-air swimming pool and its own riding stables.

After the Second World War Chalfont Lodge was home to a very different type of education as a leading bank's staff training centre. Both pictures, of the main building and part of the grounds, date from 1950. The building was replaced by a nursing home on the site in 1990.

After a short spell as a hotel, The Grange was bought by a community of nuns and opened as The Holy Cross School in 1929. This 1965 aerial view includes some of the many additions, now almost surrounding the original house.

St Mary's School was founded in London in 1872. In 1937, in anticipation of the war, it transferred to Orche Hill Avenue, Gerrards Cross, moving to Orche Hill House in Packhorse Road the following year. This postcard of Orche Hill House was published in about 1910.

THE TRIANGLE COLLEGE AT St. HUBERT'S, GERRARDS CROSS.

H.Q. SOUTH MOLTON STREET, LONDON, W.I.

St Huberts mansion became the war-time home of the Triangle College, evacuated from the West End of London. This card was sent by a student in 1941 who had nearly finished her training there and expected to get a job in a government office.

Six

Recuperation

Unlike most villages and small towns, Chalfont St Peter and Gerrards Cross were provided with an excellent Cottage Hospital as early as 1871, thanks to the generosity of a local land-owner. The Chalfonts and Gerrards Cross Hospital was built on a plot near the bottom of Gold Hill, central to the three parishes it served, all at the expense of the Hibbert family of Chalfont Park. Initially with six beds and a cot, and staffed by one medical officer and a nurse, it was extended in 1924, and again in 1926 to meet the requirements of the post-railway increase in population. To cope with the still growing demand for treatment a scheme was launched in 1927 to double the size again, and this drawing of the proposed final building formed the cover of a booklet appealing for funds.

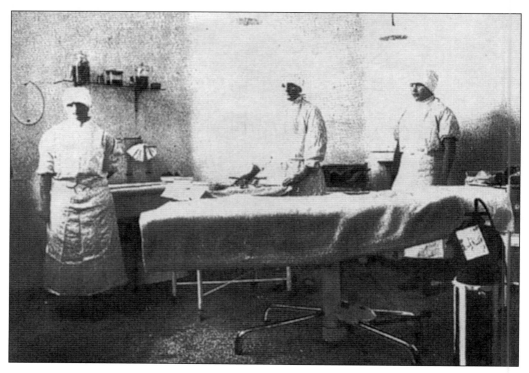

This picture, also from the appeal brochure, is of the Hospital's octagonal operating theatre, which dates from the 1924 extension.

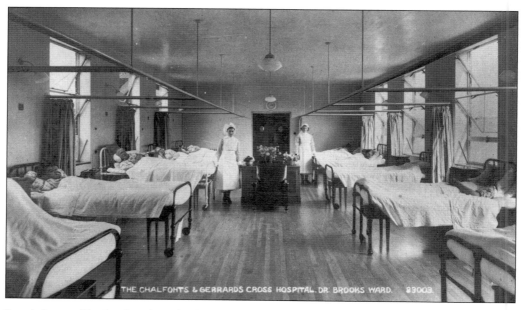

THE CHALFONTS & GERRARDS CROSS HOSPITAL. DR. BROOKS WARD. 83003

Local doctor Charles Brooks, who lived on Gold Hill, was the Hospital's Medical Officer and consulting surgeon from about 1900 until the mid twenties, and this ward in the 1928 extension was named after him.

Photographed in about 1930, this is the Hospital with its completed extension, viewed from the entrance drive. The building beside the main door still contained the operating theatre.

Pictured in 1900, The Pilgrim's Home, housing fifteen aged persons, was built on the edge of Gerrards Cross Common in 1874 by Sir John Alexander in memory of Sir William Alexander. The Tudor-style building with a typically Victorian brick garden wall and matching pump house, was also endowed with £250 per annum for its upkeep.

Later managed and maintained by The Aged Pilgrim's Friend Society, whose London headquarters published this postcard after the Second World War, the attractive building with its spectacular chimney-stacks served its original purpose for many years until converted into eight separate dwellings, now re-named Hartley Court.

The Colony, the Chalfont Home of the National Society for the Employment of Epileptics, opened in 1894 when the Society bought Skippings Farm at the northern end of Chalfont St Peter and erected a temporary iron building. Many separate houses were then built over the following years, eventually reaching a total of some two dozen. This 1920 postcard shows the wooded grounds in which the houses were built.

All the individually-designed houses were occupied by their own groups of colonists, and each had its own separate staff. Here the patients (colonists) and staff of Eleanor Home pose outside their front door in about 1910.

Most of the male colonists found healthy employment on the 150 acres of farmland surrounding the Homes. The fields, orchards, and market garden produced all the Homes' fruit and vegetable requirements and the surplus provided a useful income for the Society. This 1912 postcard shows colonists gathering potatoes in the colony's fields.

Many of the women colonists were employed in the Society's laundry, while others worked in the central kitchen, shown here in a 1912 photograph.

When no longer needed for accommodation, the original temporary building was converted into a maintenance centre for the estate with painters' and carpenters' shops and a forge. The three blacksmiths are pictured here in about 1910.

Although those who were able to do so, were expected to pull their weight, life was not all work, and the multi-purpose recreation hall was used for church services, exhibitions, and other forms of entertainment. Here, the small but adequate stage is set out for a play performed by a group of colonists, for the benefit of their colleagues.

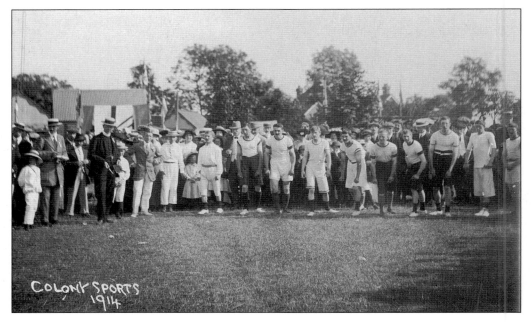

Outdoor recreation was also encouraged, with football pitches and tennis lawns, and annual sports days were organized. This photograph shows the cross-country runners awaiting the starting signal on the 1914 sports day.

On the southern edge of Gerrards Cross, beyond the Oxford Road, St Huberts was built in 1847 for the Reid sisters, known later as the benefactors of the church. Pictured here in 1910, it was then owned by Colonel the Honourable William le Poer Trench who opened the mansion, during the summer months, as St Lawrence's Convalescent Home for Children.

Seven

Recreation

Leaving aside hunting, the earliest recorded sporting activity in the area was horse-racing at Gerrards Cross in 1734. This chapter includes buildings and grounds associated either directly or indirectly with leisure activities or other forms of entertainment and relaxation in the twentieth century. Again starting this selection at the extreme end of Chalfont St Peter in the separate little hamlet of Horn Hill, the Village Hall was given and endowed in the twenties by the owners of Newland Park, whose estate then included much of Horn Hill. This photograph of the attractive building was taken within a few years of its completion.

Moving further along the ridge between the Misbourne and Colne Valleys, the Chalfont Heights Scout Camp, on the high ground at the top of Hogtrough Wood, is pictured here in around 1950. Catering mainly for scout parties from London, other parts of the wooded site include a small stream running through a clearing in the trees. More permanent facilities added later include a swimming pool.

Coming nearer to the village, the Gerrards Cross Golf Links, pictured in 1930, were first laid out in 1921, in one of the loveliest places 'in the neighbourhood, the grounds of Chalfont Park', primarily for the use of guests at the hotel there, with both a 9-hole and an 18-hole course.

Among the other facilities available within Chalfont Park were fishing and a limited amount of shooting, seen on a 1915 postcard of The Fir Tunnel, a popular feature of the dense plantation on the slopes above the waterfall.

Seen at the centre of this late twenties aerial photograph, Chalfont St Peter's War Memorial Hall, a pair of ex-army huts, had opened in 1920 on the corner of Gold Hill Lane and Church Lane, for whist drives, dances and other social events. One of the huts was fitted out in 1930 as the Broadway cinema, which remained in use for over twenty years. It was demolished and replaced by the final block of Market Place shops in 1962.

Near the top of Gold Hill, but actually in neighbouring Chalfont St Giles parish, is Chalfont Grove, which has a long history involving the early Quakers. Pictured in 1905, the house later became the headquarters of the Army Kinema Corporation, which, through several changes of name and technology, continues to originate news, entertainment and information programmes for British servicemen overseas.

In Gerrards Cross, the Playhouse cinema opened in 1925 in Ethorpe Crescent, a newly created road on the former grounds of Ethorpe House. In this 1945 photograph from Ethorpe Close looking towards Packhorse Road and Station Road, the back of the cinema, which fills the right hand side of the view, is unidentified, all advertising being reserved for the other side of the building, where it is visible from the main shopping centre.

The stables of the old rectory on East Common were converted in 1922 as a Memorial to the men of Gerrards Cross who died in the Great War. Pictured in 1930, the new building, 'an elegant pavilion with a portico sheltering a handsome war memorial', contained a billiard room, a kitchen and two other meeting rooms, with adjacent bowling green and tennis courts.

The Vicarage itself was converted after the Second World War as The Memorial Centre, photographed in the early fifties. It houses the Gerrards Cross Community Association, which also serves as an umbrella organization for over fifty affiliated local societies, offering a modern hall with stage, offices, meeting rooms and a members bar.

69

St. Hubert's Cottages, Gerrards Cross.

At the end of East Common, the block of St Huberts Cottages was built in the 1860s with a public reading room in the middle of the terrace under the decorative turret. Here, for a small subscription, local residents could catch up on the weekly publications or borrow from the library's selection of 120 books. This photograph, with a line-up of the latest automobiles outside the reading room, dates from the early thirties.

Gerrards Cross Common provided ample scope for quiet enjoyment, picnics and other informal relaxation. In this 1900 photograph, when the common was mostly open, with clumps of gorse and heather, two of the three ladies are picking wild flowers while the third looks after two children in a high Victorian perambulator.

It is unusual to find an area of water without junior fishermen, and Latchmoor Pond is no exception. In this 1915 view of the corner of the pond, five boys with improvised fishing rods stand hopefully at the water's edge, with a bucket ready for any fish they may catch.

71

Founded in 1882, the Gerrards Cross Cricket Club played on an area of the common opposite the Bull Hotel, where, for each game, they had to erect a marquee as a pavilion. At the wicket they also had to compete with the grazing cattle, seen on the unfenced pitch area beyond the gorse in this 1900 view.

The Cricket Pavilion, Gerrard's Cross.

In 1914 the Cricket Club moved to a borrowed field behind St James Church, moving again after The Great War to their own ground in Dukes Wood where they erected a proper pavilion, pictured.

Eight
'Peter's Chalfont'

An early twentieth–century guide records that the local residents still referred to the old village as 'Peter's Chalfont' (often pronounced Chaffont), a version of the name also found on some early maps. This chapter features some of the old parts of the village, and all the pictures date from the first few years of the twentieth century (except where otherwise noted), starting at the northern extremity of the Parish and working generally south towards Gerrards Cross. Newland Park was bought in 1770 by Henry Thomas Gott, an extremely wealthy man who rebuilt the house and redesigned the garden. He was a very keen huntsman who numbered royalty among his hunting cronies. Two centuries later, with much additional building in the grounds, Newland Park became the Buckinghamshire College.

Pictured in 1910, Gott's Monument was erected in about 1785 as a way-marker for important visitors to Newland Park, beside the lane which was later to become the main entrance to the Chalfont Colony. The ill-fated flint structure needed repair only four years later and was reduced to half its original height when struck by lightning in 1964.

This is the junction of Gravel Hill, the continuation of Chalfont St Peter High Street and the main road to Amersham, dropping down to the left, with Rickmansworth Lane on the right, which climbs to Chalfont Common and The Colony. In the centre, between the two roads is Hill House, built in 1800 for Samuel Acton, the grandly titled 'Surveyor to the Commissioners of the Sewers of London'.

GRAVEL HILL, CHALFONT ST PETER

The Village from the North, Chalfont St. Peter.

Entering High Street, this was the view into the village centre where, since 1968 a widened road and a large roundabout have replaced nearly all of the pictured buildings. The only survivor today is the block in the distance, behind the well-loaded cart.

Chalfont St Peters.

Another view of the old buildings sacrificed in 1966 for road improvements, this photograph was taken from the corner of Joiners Lane (the edge of today's roundabout), looking back towards Gravel Hill. At the right edge of the view, the attractive Kings Arms Hotel, with its prominent bay window, stood at the foot of Joiners Lane.

Immediately behind the Kings Arms in Joiners Lane was a run-down cottage, the ancient smithy, and then Forge House, the home of the blacksmith and his family, seen standing outside the forge in this picture.

In this view of the forge, the blacksmith is shoeing a horse outside in the lane. The old building collapsed before the Second World War, but the family business, by then mostly wrought iron work, continued in nearby premises, and in 1953 they made the frame for the Coronation Clock on Gold Hill.

HIGH ST. FROM S.W. CHALFONT ST. PETER. 1175.

In the centre of the village, this 1910 view back past the churchyard railings toward the distant Kings Arms, includes a large group of children on the newly built road bridge over the Misbourne, while a horse and cart prefer to use the remaining ford. Behind the youngsters three of the village's early shops, a baker's, a haberdasher's and a butcher's adjoin the George Inn.

Now looking the other way across a deserted village centre the newly bridged stream flows between two more of the village shops, run by Mr and Mrs Brown. His hardware store stood to the left of the stream, with storage sheds built over the water, and her grocery store to the right. Both were replaced in the sixties by modern shop buildings.

Key's Grocery Stores and Post Office, Chalfont St. Peter.

Keys Grocery was next to the churchyard, with the Post Office alongside. This card was used by Mr Keys in 1906 to order two sides of bacon from Smithfield Market, and the picture includes the owner in the shop doorway, with a telegram delivery boy on his bike outside.

Next to the Post Office, these two sixteenth century cottages were a genuine 'bit of old Chalfont St Peter' which remained until demolition in the thirties. The right hand cottage had been converted into a barber shop for Mr Herrlein, who also published many of the early postcards of the village.

On the opposite side of High Street, Greens saddlery displayed a selection of its wares outside on the pavement and hanging from the porch. The open door of the adjacent cottage led into the front room, where Mrs Herrlein, the barber's wife, sold toys and novelties.

"A Bit of Old Chalfont St Peter."

Chalfont St Peter, Looking North.

A little further along the road, the old cottages on the right of this view backed onto Barrack Yard, a square of ancient cottages leading down to the Misbourne. Barrack Yard was demolished just before the Second World War but the memorial garden planned for the site was never built. After the war the High Street cottages were also demolished and all were replaced by a typical block of ugly modern shops.

Further again and now past the oldest part of the village, these Victorian cottages in the High Street were still fairly young when photographed. They were allowed to remain, but all have now been converted into shops.

Chalfont St Peter High Street leads into the Lower Road to Gerrards Cross, running along the western boundary of Chalfont Park. This lodge and ornate gates which protected the southern drive to the mansion disappeared in the sixties under the concrete and tarmac of the bypass. The house, one of the historic manor houses of the district, was rebuilt in its present form for the Churchill family in 1755, and later given fancy Victorian decorations.

Chalfont House, Chalfont St. Peter.

The estate was owned by a succession of wealthy families before becoming a hotel. In 1944 it was bought by a national company as a research centre and now houses the company's head offices.

HOME FARM. CHALFONT PARK. BUCKS.

Previously known as Coldharbour, the Home Farm of the Chalfont Park Estate is sheltered by Coldharbour Wood and the ornamental Round Copse on the slopes above Chalfont Park's lake.

Nine
Gold Hill and Austenwood

Continuing the tour of the oldest parts of the district, this chapter portrays the old buildings and open scenery on and around Gold Hill and Austenwood Commons, the open spaces which separated Chalfont St Peter from Gerrards Cross. Starting from Chalfont St Peter, Gold Hill Lane climbs from the middle of the High Street up to the common. At the turn of the century John Bishop opened his 'Popular Stores' at the foot of the lane, selling groceries and hardware from the shop built on to the front of his cottage, and all manner of new and second-hand goods and furniture from the wooden warehouse next door. This card was published for Bishops in about 1905.

Beyond Bishops and the neighbouring greengrocers and garage, the rough Gold Hill Lane climbed between the grounds of The Grange, behind the trees on the left, and an area of allotments protected by the wooden fence. Pictured in about 1900, Gold Hill Lane later became Market Place, the main shopping street of Chalfont St Peter.

A little further uphill, the lane divides along the north and east sides of the triangular Gold Hill Common, and this 1905 view is from the bottom corner looking back across the valley to Chalfont Common in the misty distance, with the hospital and school buildings on the near slope.

Continuing up Gold Hill North, this photograph was taken just after the Great War from the gorse-covered Common, with a belt of trees hiding the village. The magnificent tree to the left of the picture stood at the entrance to Dell Farm in its sheltered hollow, surrounded by orchards which were soon to be lost to housing development.

From the north west corner of the Common, Layters Green Lane runs through farmland and open countryside to the Oxford Road between Gerrards Cross and Beaconsfield. The tree-lined pond in this 1900 view borders the lane a short distance from Gold Hill.

Returning to the south-east side of Gold Hill Common, The Grange, described in a 1904 guide as 'An agreeable modern country house' was built on the site of the seventeenth century home of a leading Quaker family, which had then been the unofficial meeting place for local members of the Society of Friends, when their gatherings were against the law.

The Chestnuts, Gold Hill, Chalfont St. Peter.

Uphill, beyond the Grange estate, this group of early nineteenth century cottages lines the edge of the Common, partly behind a trio of fine trees. The title of this 1910 postcard refers not to the trees, but to the name of the detached house at the far end of the cottages, the only casualty of later development apart from the pond which was filled in in 1938.

At the southern, top, corner of Gold Hill Common, a line of simple cottages dating from the eighteenth and early nineteenth centuries leads up to the Victorian Baptist chapel. This 1900 photograph of the cottages and chapel includes a group of worshippers on their way home to the village.

Austenwood Lane extends from the chapel corner of Gold Hill Common to Gerrards Cross, and this late twenties view looking back towards Gold Hill includes some of the post-railway development which started to join the two villages.

Further along Austenwood Lane in about 1905, the group of cattle is heading towards Gerrards Cross, while the two separate cows are on the path across the common to Bull Lane. School Lane runs from the direction post along the crest to the right before descending to the Lower Road.

Opposite: Adjoining the chapel on its other side, this cottage, pictured in 1905, was the first of a short terrace which was later demolished for road widening, an extension to the chapel, and as a site for the manse.

Looking towards Gerrards Cross from the same road junction in the twenties, the lane has been widened and surfaced, with a pavement to serve the new houses facing the Common. The steep bank in front of the farmhouse is a result of mineral extraction, while beyond the farm the site of a former brickworks had already been developed as part of The Firs Estate.

Holly Tree Farm's ancient timber-framed farmhouse is shown here in about 1905. In addition to the adjoining barn, there are further farm buildings in the walled-in area of Austenwood Common behind the house.

Ten

'Jarret's Cross'

In previous centuries the cross-roads was known as Jarret's or Jarred's Cross, but there is no definite identification of either Jarret or Gerrard. Apart from a couple of farms and a few large houses and their parklands, pre-railway Gerrards Cross consisted of only a handful of cottages, inns and shops round the common, some of which are pictured in this chapter. Almost all these pictures, many from the same, unidentified photographer, date from between 1900 and 1906, at which date Gerrards Cross contained only seventy-five dwellings. Following on from Austenwood Lane, Packhorse Road runs alongside the extensive grounds of Orche Hill, past the Packhorse Inn to the Oxford Road cross-roads, continuing as the Windsor Road. In this 1920 photograph the original Orche Hill Lodge is the only visible building although Packhorse Road was one of the first Edwardian developments, but all the new houses were set well back from the road behind mature trees.

Towards the end of the East Common, this view from a patch of gorse over a grassy corner of the Common, includes the eighteenth and early nineteenth century cottages next to St Huberts, all of which are now listed buildings.

At the south-eastern tip of Gerrards Cross Common, where the road now known as East Common meets the Oxford Road, this view includes, from left to right, part of St Huberts Cottages, the Fox and Hounds Inn (now The Apple Tree) and, on the other side of the main road, The French Horn.

Now a closer view of the whole block of St Huberts Cottages, eight dwellings with the public reading room in the centre, built in 1866. They are believed to have been built for Mayne Reid, who started building his own mansion beside the Oxford Road the same year.

This block, near the corner of Mill Lane, contains one of Gerrards Cross' earliest shops, Henry Bonsey's butchers business, with all its domestic windows protected by striped canvas sun-blinds.

This large house, set back from the edge of the Common to the west of Mill Lane, and with lodges guarding its two entrance gates, was built in 1821. Originally known as Walters Croft, it became The Vicarage some seventy years later.

Pictured in 1915, this path across the common links the vicarage to the church. An additional connection was made early in the century, during the incumbency of Revd John Glubb, when a private telephone cable was laid under the path to allow his invalid wife to hear his services without leaving her room.

Some way behind the church and just off the Windsor Road, Manor Farm, pictured in 1905 with its adjacent barn and stables, was situated in a forty acre clearing within the woods of Bulstrode Park. Its fields, together with much of the woodland were later developed as the Dukes Wood Estate.

Returning to the crossroads, this pond lies in the corner of west common between the Oxford Road and Packhorse Road. In this picture it was open to the Oxford Road and the houses opposite, but is now surrounded by scrub so dense that most users of the main road are unaware of its existence.

Back in Packhorse Road at the entrance to the modern village centre, the partly hidden Packhorse Inn stands to the left of the road with a large advertisement for Wellers, the Amersham Brewery, above the adjoining former smithy in this 1900 photograph.

West from The Packhorse, which is just visible at the end of the road, the common was edged with well-separated pairs and groups of Victorian cottages. In this 1915 photograph, the nearest block is Langstones Villas, two of which, together with two neighbouring cottages, were still occupied by members of the Langstone family until after the Second World War.

Further west we come to the almost separate little community of Latchmoor, where all the houses in this 1900 view are now listed buildings. The most prominent of these was Latchmoor House, now re-named Walpole House, a seventeenth century farm cottage with added Georgian façade.

Between the houses and the pond, which was man-made some time before the eighteenth century, is a narrow track which continued as a footpath across the fields back to Austenwood Common. In this view, posted in 1905, a queue of assorted wagons appears to be gathering on the track.

Directly facing the water at the back of the pond, Latchmoor Cottage, like its neighbours, dates from the turn of the nineteenth century. At the edge of the pond, where the bank slopes gently into the water, a group of children stand quietly watching the lad with the fishing rod.

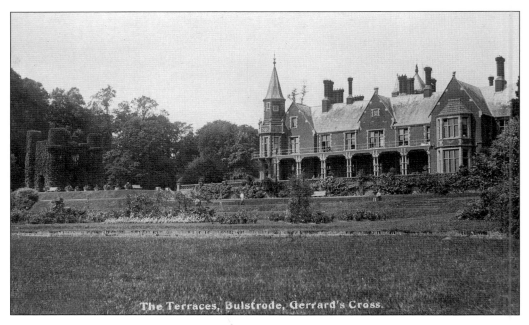

The Terraces, Bulstrode, Gerrard's Cross.

Opposite the western end of the common was one of the main entrances to Bulstrode Park, the historic estate which covered over a square mile of former heathland south of the Oxford Road, including a prehistoric hill-fort, the top of which was the only level ground in the whole area. The original medieval house was replaced in the seventeenth century and a second replacement in the nineteenth took over fifty years to complete. The south front and part of the entrance gateway are all that now remain of this succession of buildings.

Eleven

The Railway

The Great Western and Great Central Railway's joint line through Gerrards Cross, the last railway to be built through Buckinghamshire, opened in April 1906 after an army of over 200 navvies had invaded the area for nearly four years during its construction. In the immediate vicinity of Chalfont St Peter and Gerrards Cross the undulating ground necessitated massive civil engineering works, including a cutting through the Chiltern chalk some forty-five feet deep and well over a mile long. It is pictured here in 1905 from the Chalfont St Peter end, where the ground falls away to the Misbourne valley, with temporary tracks for the contractor's trains removing the spoil from the excavations.

Some of the heavy excavation work was done by the latest engineering aid, the steam cutter or 'navvy', ten of which were employed on this section of line together with the human navvies and a multitude of horses to haul away the wagon-loads of spoil. This photograph of one of the machines at work in the Gerrards Cross cutting was taken in 1905.

The deep valley of the Misbourne was spanned by a long viaduct in two sections with an embankment in between, all of which was completed in 1905. One section is pictured here in that year from the Lower Road, with a temporary light-weight bridge for construction traffic still in place behind the main brick arches.

Great Western & Great Central
Railway Viaduct,
Near Gerrard's Cross.

This 1907 view from the Chalfont St Peter side of the valley shows both sections of the viaduct. Behind the dark tree is the massive embankment separating the distant arches spanning the Misbourne from the right hand section over the Uxbridge to Chalfont Road.

In this 1907 view across the new station deep in its cutting, the embryo shopping centre can be seen on the far bank, with Station Parade facing the drive up from the station, and a further block of Packhorse Road shops behind the trees to the left.

To prevent anyone from abusing the privilege of access, the joint railway company ensured the privacy of their approach road to Gerrards Cross Station with this notice at the top, where it joins Packhorse Road. Beyond the station entrance, which is at first floor level, the drive continued on down to track level for the goods yard.

Looking from the other bank in 1908, the first houses of Bulstrode Way line the edge of the cutting. The area of cattle pens at the track side indicates the amount of animal traffic expected here.

Gerrards Cross Station.

Another picture from the early years of the railway, this track-level view emphasises the extreme width of the cutting here, with a local train to High Wycombe pulling into the station on the slow track. The station's passenger accommodation and booking office are on the first floor of the main building, opening directly onto the footbridge on one side and the approach drive on the other.

The two middle tracks through the station allowed express trains to pass the slower locals. Pictured here on 10 April 1926, the 2.10 p.m. from Paddington to Birkenhead, headed by GWR locomotive *Rob Roy* roars under the Packhorse Road bridge and through the station.

Twelve
Chalfont St Peter Shops

At the end of the nineteenth century the old village of Chalfont St Peter could already boast a fair selection of shops and businesses, with over a dozen listed in the 1895 directory, mostly in the High Street. Starting this chapter with Chalfont Common, the first picture is not strictly a shop, but Mr and Mrs Grieve at their bungalow, The Whins Cottage in Denham Lane, in the twenties, where they sold 'Valuable wood carvings, archaeological antiquities in stone and brick, and uncommon copper and brass ornaments, to be viewed by appointment only'. At one time these included exotic Hindu carvings taken from the original Juggernaut, a massive ceremonial carriage. They also sold exotic herbs, which were dried on the premises.

Chalfont Common, before the Second World War was just a scattering of well-separated houses and bungalows mainly along Chesham, Denham and Rickmansworth Lanes. It developed rapidly in the fifties, when this corner shop and Post Office opened at the cross-roads to serve the new residents.

This photograph of the High Street was taken in about 1930, shortly after the Misbourne had been buried under the concrete of the widened road. For many years Bridge House, the tall early Victorian building facing The Greyhound, had housed the first shops of the village's shopping centre.

Also from about 1930, this photograph was taken from outside The Greyhound, looking past the last exposed part of the Misbourne into the main part of High Street. Howard Roberts, the local chain of high-class grocery shops, had recently taken over the large shop premises opposite the church.

In the middle of High Street, two long-established shops still stood on either side of the Gold Hill Lane junction in the twenties. The ladies with the pram are outside the premises of Mr F Ranschart who sold, hired, and repaired cycles and motorcycles, while Harris's sweet shop (then still known to the locals as Kemps, the previous proprietors) occupies the opposite corner.

Looking into the continuation of High Street in the thirties, the corner sweet shop had been demolished for road widening, leaving the next-door cottage, then Barclays Bank, as the corner. Though only open for two hours, four mornings a week, Barclay's service greatly exceeded that of rivals, The Westminster, open Monday mornings only. The corner was later rebuilt at a permanent full-time branch of Barclays.

The first major change to shopping in Chalfont St Peter came in 1923 with the construction of Market Place, the line of shops along one side only of Gold Hill Lane, facing The Grange estate, which prevented any development on that side of the road. The new shops started some way past Church Lane as the Memorial Hall occupied the first part of the site, behind the railings at the right edge of this late twenties photograph.

Looking back down the first dozen shops of Market Place in their second year, 1924, the nearest shop, A J Mills, listed in the directory specifically as a Ham and Beef dealer, has Heinz posters in his window, with a conventional butchers shop next door. A couple of doors down, the still-vacant premises provide useful off-street parking for its neighbours' delivery cycles.

Opposite: Market Place extends to the beginning of Gold Hill Common. This 1927 photograph of the whole length had been marked by the sender to identify his shop on the corner of The Vale, the only interruption to the otherwise continuous block of shops.

MARKET PLACE.
CHALFONT ST PETER

Just beyond the top of Market Place, on the edge of the Common, Glynn's tobacconists and confectioners shop, later general stores, occupied part of the cottage on the corner of Nicol Road from before the First World War until the Second.

CHALFONT ST. PETER, BUCKS.

Looking back from the Common to the top end of Market Place on a fine day in the late fifties, a prominent feature is the Coronation Clock, Chalfont St Peter's permanent memento of 1953.

Thirteen
Gerrards Cross Shops

THE OLD POST OFFICE. 301
SPAULL & CO GERRARD'S CROSS

Where now is the main shopping centre of Gerrards Cross, nothing existed prior to the construction of the railway, after which it developed very rapidly. To the north-west side of Packhorse Road was the garden of Ethorpe House, otherwise acres of open fields, and on the other side the fields of Marsham Farm. At this date the only shops to be found were on the Oxford Road and around the edge of The Common. The pictures in this chapter illustrate, in chronological sequence, the development of Gerrards Cross as a shopping centre. The original Gerrards Cross Post Office was an extension to Flint Cottage, where the Matthews family added postal duties to their well-established tailoring business on the corner of West Common facing The Bull Hotel. When pictured, in 1913, after fifty years there the postal business had just been transferred to the new building in Packhorse Road and the old post office had become The Gerrards Cross Laundry.

Pictured in about 1900, Henry Bonsey's butcher's shop had already been in business on East Common near the junction of Mill Lane for some ten years and was to remain there for a further twenty, by which time another member of the Bonsey family had opened a butchers shop in Station Road, joining a third already in business at Chalfont St Peter.

Turning now to the new shopping centre, the first shops were built in Station Road, Oak End Way and, pictured here from the railway bridge in 1907, Station Parade. Starting from the right the first three shops were then an estate agents, a cycle dealer, and a part-time branch of Barclays Bank.

Around the corner in Station Road, the first shops there were the bakery and restaurant of F. C. Moss who also published this card in 1908, and Bonsey's butchers shop in the ornate building opposite. Further along, the scattering of builders' huts indicates more work in progress.

The further end of the shopping centre is shown on this 1908 postcard, with the gardens of Ethorpe House still preventing building on the other side of Packhorse Road.

This close view of Wood's shop and restaurant on the corner of Oak End Way with the proprietor in his smartly turned out carriage, was published in 1908 as an advertisement for the confectioners' and pastrycooks' business.

Around the corner in Oak End Way, this is the view back towards the grounds of Ethorpe past the newly opened shops lining one side of the road. The trees on the other side mark the boundary of Marsham Farm, on the fields of which housing development had already started.

Looking, in 1912, from the upstairs window of Heath's drapery next to Woods in The Parade. The well-wooded grounds still hide Ethorpe House while, to the right is the handsome new building for Barclays Bank, only just completed.

By this date, development was beginning on the other side of the railway, but not immediately next to the lines. The first building, photographed in 1912 looking back to the bridge, was the new Post Office, still only a sub-office, shared with the tailor's shop on the corner of Marsham Way.

A couple of years later, the Post Office had moved across Marsham Way to this prominent new main office on the other corner. Pictured in 1918, more shops had also been built next to their previous premises, back towards the railway bridge.

Pictured here in about 1920, the next development was a parade of shops in Packhorse Road on the other side from the Post Office, and extending toward The Packhorse.

Now an early twenties close-up of one of the new shops between the Post Office and the railway bridge, the premises of Reginald Allen, ladies and gentlemen's tailor.

Returning across the railway. By 1921 the last gap in Station Parade had been filled by the London Country and Westminster Bank on the corner of Station Road, but Ethorpe House still prevented building on the other side of the road.

By the mid–twenties, shops had been built along the whole of the former Ethorpe land, pictured here in about 1932 when Station Garage had taken over the three shops facing Station Approach and added petrol pumps at the road-side.

Fourteen
'Genteel Residences'

In the second half of the nineteenth century, the newly created parish of Gerrards Cross was described as 'A very respectable place with many genteel residences'. The post-railway developers who created the village as we now know it did their very best to maintain those standards, with individually architect-designed houses mostly on large plots. At the same time Chalfont St Peter, its long-established neighbour, also started to grow, but generally with less opulent properties. Even before completion of the railway, new roads had been laid out on both sides of the Gerrards Cross cutting and construction of the first houses of the Latchmoor Estate was well under way. This drawing of a typical house on the new estate is taken from an advertising brochure of 1906.

Latchmoor Estate, Gerrard's X from Railway Foot-Bridge.

The long railway cutting separated Bulstrode Way and Orchehill Avenue, the two principal roads of the Latchmoor Estate. However this footbridge, pictured in 1908, provided a direct connection for pedestrians.

Photographed in 1910, Bulstrode Way, on the former fields of Latchmoor Farm, was then virtually fully developed with just the odd gap where building on a plot had been delayed.

Opposite: The former parkland of the Orche Hill Estate was next to be developed, in two stages. North Park, advertised here in 1907, was followed by the other half, South Park, a couple of years later.

The finest Sites in this charming neighbourhood
are situate at

NORTH PARK

with beautiful views over the Misbourne Valley
and Chalfont Park.

Gravel Soil.   Gas and Electric Light.   Company's Water.
Bracing Air.   Low Rates.

Development of the North Park Estate spread with the construction of Kings Waye leading towards Chalfont St Peter along the line of a former field path. The newly built houses of Kings Waye are shown on this 1908 postcard.

Off Kings Waye, Austen Way and The Ridgway were also constructed before 1910, and this 1920 photograph is of the fashionably furnished lounge of 'Kia-Ora', one of the houses on The Ridgway.

Houses in South Park, the second part of the Orche Hill Estate, were offered by a local builder from 1910, with more large properties, well screened by mature trees and separated by an informal road layout. Part of South Park is pictured here in 1912.

Meanwhile, in Chalfont St Peter, construction of the Common Downs Estate started after the arrival of the railway in the area had created an unprecedented demand for more houses. The Estate, which eventually covered much of the high ground above the hospital and to the north of Gold Hill, is pictured from the air in about 1927, with Market Place across the top right corner and Lansdown Road across the middle of the view.

High Street, Chalfont St.

In the late twenties the fields beside and above the southern end of Chalfont St Peter High Street, towards the North Park Estate were developed. In this 1930 view of the High Street looking back towards the centre of the village, the publisher seems to have forgotten which of the Chalfonts his photographer had visited.

Acknowledgements

I am very grateful to Julian Hunt, Buckinghamshire's Heritage Manager, for providing from the County Museum Collection the picture of Gerrards Cross cinema, and to Pam Everett for the loan of the Chalfont St Peter Church of England School group. All the other pictures are taken from postcards, books and photographs in my own collection, and I express my sincere thanks to the original photographers, mostly anonymous, and the publishers who made their work more widely available. I would also like to thank those, both visitors and residents, who bought the postcards and sent them to their friends who, in turn, saved them for many years in their own collections before they appeared on the market again.

I also acknowledge my gratitude to the authors of guidebooks, whose works have been quoted or consulted for historical detail.

All the earlier pictures are now out of copyright, but the position is unclear with regard to the more recent illustrations, and I apologise here to any copyright owners who have not been consulted.